DATE DUE

Principles of Currency:
THE BANK CHARTER ACT OF 1844

Also published in

Reprints of Economic Classics

by John E. Cairnes

The Character and Logical Method of Political Economy [1875]

Essays in Political Economy [1873]

Political Essays [1873]

The Slave Power [1863]

Some Leading Principles of Political Economy Newly Expounded [1874]

AN

EXAMINATION

INTO THE

PRINCIPLES OF CURRENCY

INVOLVED IN THE

BANK CHARTER ACT OF 1844

BY

·JOHN E. CAIRNES

[1854]

Reprints of Economic Classics

AUGUSTUS M. KELLEY · PUBLISHERS
NEW YORK · 1966

LIBRARY OF CONGRESS CATALOGUE CARD NUMBER

65 - 20924

AN EXAMINATION

INTO THE

PRINCIPLES OF CURRENCY

INVOLVED IN THE

BANK CHARTER ACT OF 1844.

BY

JOHN E. CAIRNES, ESQ., A.M.

_____

DUBLIN:

HODGES AND SMITH, 104, GRAFTON STREET,
Booksellers to the University.

LONDON: RIDGEWAY, PICCADILLY.

—

1854.

[*Price One Shilling.*]

THE substance of the following pamphlet was read before the Dublin Statistical Society, on the 19th of June last. Owing to the importance which the subject treated of has lately assumed, from the state of our relations with foreign countries, and the disturbing influence which these are likely to exercise on monetary affairs ; and, considering the probability of the Bank Charter being shortly subjected to a revision, it has been thought advisable, (with the permission of the Council of the Dublin Statistical Society, under whose sanction it is published)* to add to the paper, as originally read, some new matter, and to expand and illustrate more fully the principles advanced, with a view to rendering them more generally intelligible.

June, 1854.

---

* It is not to be understood that, in sanctioning the publication of a work, the Society pledges itself to all the opinions contained in it.

AN EXAMINATION,

&c.

THE prospects of the country at the present moment, on the opening of a European war, present many aspects of anxious interest, and afford indications of a revival of many subjects of discussion, as well of an economical and financial as of a political character, which have long been allowed to slumber in silence. Amongst these we may expect to find our monetary laws pretty severely canvassed ; and it is certain that the necessity of supporting large military expenditure in foreign countries is a circumstance of precisely that kind which is likely to bring these laws to a severe test. We have already parted with some four or five millions of bullion in discharge of foreign liabilities of one kind or another ; and though the exchanges may have rallied for the present, it is not possible that the country should carry on its warlike proceedings on the scale which seems to be contemplated, without becoming subject to occasional drains of the precious metals of a more extensive character than we have for many years experienced. The occasion, therefore, seems not to be unsuitable for inviting public attention to a consideration of the principles upon which our currency laws are based. These principles, so far at least as regards the control of our paper circulation, are embodied in the Bank Charter Act of 1844. Into all the provisions of that Act it is not intended in the following observations to enter : the points which it is proposed to discuss are those only which affect the central establishment in London ; according to which an artificial limit, prescribed by the legislature, is placed upon the issue of notes payable on demand.

The projects which have been brought forward at different times for the regulation of the currency have been various, and the questions which it involves are still, perhaps, amongst the most vexed within the field of political economy. Various, however, and conflicting as are the views entertained by the highest authorities upon many points connected with the regulation of the currency, the discussion to which the question has given rise seems yet to have been productive of this one settled conclusion—I allude, of course, to the principle that paper-money should be made by law payable on demand into the gold which it professes to represent. I say, settled conclusion; because, though there are undoubtedly still some dissentients from this principle, yet it will scarcely be maintained that their authority is of such weight as to be even capable of appreciation, though tried in the most delicate balance against the names which may be adduced in support of the doctrine of "convertibility";—names which include all the most distinguished economists in the three kingdoms, all the first practical financiers, and, I believe, every statesman of eminence. A principle which, after so long a discussion, such authorities, so various and independent, have all concurred in adopting, may, it appears to me, be fairly considered as placed beyond the domain of "open questions." I am therefore, I conceive, absolved from the necessity of re-opening a controversy already, so far as argument and experiment can go, fully decided; nor shall I tax the time and patience of the reader by entering into an examination of those numerous hopeful schemes for the regeneration of society, based upon the principle of " coining the whole land of the country into money" and the like;—great and comprehensive measures, of which it has been said the process " begins in the vat of the paper mill, and ends in the desk of the counting-house."

The changes effected in our monetary system by the act of 1844 are thus stated by Mr. M'Culloch:—*
" Sir Robert Peel adopted, in dealing with the Bank of England, the proposal made by Mr. Lloyd in 1837, for effecting a complete separation between the issuing and banking departments of that establishment.

---

* M'Culloch's *Smith's Wealth of Nations*, note, p. 505.

And while the directors are left at liberty to manage the latter at discretion, their management of the former or issue department is subjected to what seems to be a well-devised system of restraint. The Bank is allowed to issue £14,000,000 of notes upon securities (of which the debt of £11,015,100 lent by her to government is a part) ; and whatever paper the issue department may at any time issue over and above this maximum amount of securities, it must have an equal amont of coin and bullion in its coffers. Hence it is impracticable for the issue department to increase its issues, without at the same time proportionally increasing its stock of coin and bullion ; or to diminish the latter without proportionally diminishing the amount of paper supplied to the public or the bank department."

The change is thus twofold ; 1st. the separation of the issue and banking departments, and 2ndly, the restriction of the issue of notes upon securities to £14,000,000, requiring for all beyond that amount an equivalent in gold to be held in the coffers of the Bank.

With regard to the separation of departments, I do not know that it is necessary to make any lengthened remark : it appears not to go beyond a question of account, and is so understood by Mr. Morris, the Governor of the Bank of England.* In point of fact the separation of the accounts took place in the year

---

* See Mr. Morris's evidence before the Secret Committee (House of Commons) on Commercial Distress, 1848.   Q. 3690.

1840, four years before the passing of the Bank Charter Act. A certain amount of notes was issued against securities and a certain amount against bullion, and the amounts were kept as separate as they have been since the act came into force.*

* The separation of the issuing and banking departments of the Bank of England has been regarded by some high authorities as leading to practical consequences of very injurious tendency, calculated directly to defeat the object for which the restriction upon the issue of notes was introduced. The practical object kept in view in that restriction was undoubtedly to impose such a check upon the proceedings of the bank as to induce it, in times of speculative excitement, to limit more narrowly than it had previously done its accommodation to the public,—to restrain, in a word, as far as possible, the spirit of overtrading. Now the effect of the separation of the departments has been, in the opinion of the authorities referred to (Mr. Horsley Palmer, Mr. Samuel Gurney, and others), to impress the bank directors with the notion that they were henceforth absolved from all responsibility to the public in their mode of management, and were bound merely to consider the pecuniary interest of their own proprietary ; and the consequence of this impression on the part of the directors has been, to induce them to deal with their reserve in such a manner as to afford, in times when speculation was rife, every encouragement and facility to the prevalent mania. It is certainly true that, before the passing of the Bank Charter Act, the directors did consider that they had something more to attend to than the dividends of the proprietors; sufficient proof of this is to be found in the general steadiness (previous to the year 1844) of the bank rate of interest, which, whatever the market rate of interest might be, was never reduced below 4 nor raised above 6 per cent ; and it is equally certain that since the passing of the act of 1844, the impression alluded to on the part of the Directors—that they were free from all obligation but that of attending to the dividends of the proprietors—did exist, and in practice governed their conduct. This, besides being established by the evidence of directors of the bank, is placed beyond doubt by their management of the bank concerns in the years 1846-7 ; when, instead of confining themselves within the limits in all previous times acted on, they entered fully into all the competition of the money market, forcing accommodation on the public when their reserve happened to be high, on such terms as two per cent. interest, and, when their reserves ran low, coming to an abrupt stop, and refusing accommodation upon any terms. That such has been the operation of the Bank Charter Act is, I conceive, placed beyond doubt, though I think it may be doubted if this effect is to be attributed to that portion of the measure

The second and more important provision, however, of the act, which restricts the issue of notes upon securities to £14,000,000, obliging the Bank for all beyond that amount to hold an equivalent quantity of gold, will require a more lengthened discussion.

The theoretical view upon which this regulation proceeds is that, in a mixed currency like ours, composed partly of coin and partly of notes, the circulation, to be perfect, should vary in the same way as it would do if the whole currency were metallic ; and this object the framers of the Act undertook more or less completely to accomplish, by providing that the amount of notes issued should rise and fall exactly as the treasure in the coffers of the Bank, (or, in other words, as the gold in the country) increased or dimi-

which provided for the separation of the issuing and banking departments, which appears to have been, on the whole, a convenient arrangement, and was practically acted on before the passing of the Bank Charter Act. The impression alluded to, with reference to the independence of the Bank in relation to the public and the injurious consequences in the management of the banking affairs to which it led, would appear to me to be more properly charged upon the other portion of the measure, which takes out of the hands of the Bank all discretion as to the control of its issues. It was inculcated by those who recommended the measure of 1844, that the issue of paper money was not properly a function of banking at all, and that, this being taken out of the hands of the Bank of England, they had thenceforward nothing to consider but the interest of the Bank as a pecuniary investment. The mischievous effects, therefore, resulting from this understanding, form a fair ground of objection, in addition to those which will be advanced in the subsequent part of this paper, against the principle of restriction contained in the act. It is quite vain to say, as has been said, that the interests of the Bank of England and those of the public, properly understood, are identical. This may be so ; but it is quite certain that the management of an establishment conducted professedly with a view to public interests, and that of one conducted professedly with a view to the interests of the proprietary alone, would be very different.

nished. Meeting the framers of the Act upon their own ground, Mr. Fullarton has shown* that their views and arguments involve an assumption which is quite unfounded in fact ; the assumption that, under a metallic currency, the circulation *would* vary in amount with the influx and efflux of gold. He has shown, from the examples of all those countries where the currency is wholly metallic, or nearly so, that an export of gold to meet foreign payments is drawn not from the money in circulation—or at least in a very insignificant proportion from the money in circulation—but from those hoards which in such countries are always secreted to a large extent in periods of prosperity when interest is low, and which the high interest, offered when large foreign payments are to be made, invariably draws forth in sufficient quantities to meet the demand. The analogy, therefore, which the promoters of the Act of 1844 aimed at establishing, between the working of our mixed currency and that of a currency purely metallic, fails completely in the essential point. For, whereas, under a purely metallic currency, the coin in the hands of the community would not be diminished to any important extent, in the event of a foreign drain of gold, till all the reserve of unemployed gold in the country was exhausted ; the Bank Charter Act, on the contrary, interdicts the export of a single ounce of gold from the reserve treasure in the country,

---

* Fullarton on the Regulation of the Currencies, pp. 71—74.

(that reserve being, under our system of currency, in the coffers of the Bank of England) unless upon the condition that an equivalent sum in bank-notes be simultaneously withdrawn from the circulation. Thus, under the one system, a drain of gold to foreign countries must exhaust the whole reserve before it reaches the circulation ; under the other, it acts immediately and exclusively upon the circulation in the hands of the public. The analogy, therefore, which the framers of the Act aimed at establishing completely breaks down.

But, even granting the assumption made by the advocates of the present system with reference to the working of a currency purely metallic, it may still, I think, well be questioned if their theory is carried out by the act of 1844, at least in any important sense of the words used. " The efflux and influx of gold," say Mr. Lloyd and Mr. Norman,* " are the only sure tests of what would have been the variations of a circulation purely metallic;" and therefore this constitutes, according to their views, the proper rule by which to control the fluctuations of a paper circulation. But what is meant by the term "circulation"? Now, the only sense in which this term was ever (until quite a recent period) understood in such controversies, was as signifying the bank notes in the hands of the public. Since, however, the period of the framing of the Bank

---

* See their evidence before the Select Committee on Banks of Issue, 1840.

Charter Act, the promoters of that measure have resorted to a new nomenclature; with a view, as it would appear, of bringing their theory as to the regulation of the currency into harmony with the operation of the act. According to them, the term "circulation" includes, besides the bank notes in the hands of the public, the additional sum held by the bank as reserve in its banking department: they consider, in fact, as "circulation," not only all the notes outside the walls of the bank, but all the notes within the bank besides. Including this reserve of notes in the bank, the circulation varies indeed as the bullion varies—this, from the very terms of the act, is a self-evident proposition. But this sense of the word "circulation" is, I maintain, a novelty in our nomenclature, introduced by the framers of the Bank Charter Act of 1844, entirely at variance with the received signification, and perfectly useless except for the purpose of reconciling a particular theory of the currency with the operation of this measure. "I believe," says Mr. Tooke,* "that in all the pamphlets, in all the evidence, in all the speeches, in which the question of banking has been discussed, the circulation has been confined to the notes in the hands of the public. · · · · There was never such a confusion of reasoning as that which would suppose that the circulation *in posse* is part of that circulation which in any way acts upon prices." The testimony of Mr.

---

* See his evidence before Secret Committee (House of Commons) on Commercial Distress, 1848, Q. 5394.

Morris,* Governor of the Bank of England in 1848, is to the same purpose. He is asked before the Committee on Commercial Distress, 1848,—

"Would you call the notes held in reserve by the Bank circulation at all?—No; not according to the usual meaning of the term.

"You would call the notes in the hands of the public real circulation?—The general acceptation of the word "circulation" includes notes out with the public, whether they are in the pockets of individuals or in the hands of private bankers.

"But it does not include the bank reserve?—No.

"Are those notes kept actually in reserve, or is it merely a matter of account?—It is a matter of account; they are paid in and cancelled, as the Bank does not re-issue notes; when they are called for, fresh notes are issued against them."

I am warranted, therefore, in assuming that the term "circulation," in the sense in which it has been always understood in controversies of this kind, stands for the amount of notes in the hands of the public. Now, in this use of the word, how does the theory of the Bank Charter Act, that the circulation should fluctuate in amount with the fluctuations in the quantity of gold in the country, correspond with the working of the act? Here is an example taken from a comparison of the years 1846 and 1847:—

---

† See his evidence before Secret Committee (House of Commons) on Commercial Distress, 1848.   Q. 3529—3532.

	Notes with the Public.	Bullion in the Bank.
June 6th, 1846 ...	£19,857,000 ...	£15,012,000.
April 3rd, 1847 ...	£19,855,000 ...	£10,246,000.
Oct. 3rd, 1846 ...	£20,551,000 ...	£15,817,000.
Oct. 3rd, 1847 ...	£18,712,000 ...	£ 8,565,000.*

It appears from a comparison of these figures that, while between June, 1846, and April, 1847, the variation in the circulation was only to the extent of £2000, the variation during the same interval in the amount of treasure was £4,766,000. And while, between October, 1846, and October, 1847, the variation in the circulation was but £1,839,000, the variation during the same time in the amount of treasure was £7,252,000.

The act, therefore, in its practical working, is as far from fulfilling the conditions of the theory which its authors propounded and designed to give effect to, as this theory is itself destitute of support from facts.

So far with regard to the theoretical aspect of the measure. With reference, next, to the practical purport of the Bill of 1844, I find it thus clearly and succinctly set forth in a passage which I have extracted from a leading article of the *Times*, October, 1847, and which, as emanating from an able and uncompromising supporter of the measure, may be taken as an unexceptionable statement of its objects:—" Peel's bill," says the *Times*, " provides two checks" (against over-issue of paper) " 1st. the natural one, which was

* Sse evidence before Secret Committee (House of Commons) on Commercial Distress, 1848.   Page 268-9.

the only check under the old charter, viz. the Bank's actual power to fulfil its promise to pay ; and 2ndly, the artificial and arbitrary check which obliges the Bank to keep gold in its coffers for all its notes beyond £14,000,000. · · · On an average of years it appeared safe to suppose £14,000,000 of notes to be always outstanding, but not a larger sum. · · · · Under the old charter, the discretion was left to the directors ; under the new, the legislature fixed the rule of prudence."

I do not stop to inquire whether £14,000,000 is the maximum that should have been selected ; or whether, supposing it to have been justified by the state of our commercial transactions in 1844, some addition might not now be safely made to that sum under the extension which commerce has since experienced. The question to which I shall address myself is the one stated by the *Times*, and which appears to go to the root of the subject, viz. whether the issue of bank notes can be best left to the discretion—I will not say necessarily of the bank directors—but of some competent and judiciously organized body ; or whether, as the *Times* prefers, and as the Act of 1844 provides, the legislature should fix ' the rule of prudence.'

First, then, in what does the perfection of a system of currency consist, and by what criterion are we to judge of its merits ? In ordinary times, when commerce moves along in its regular and natural course, there is little room for testing the merits of a currency : it must be a bad system indeed that in quiet times fails to adapt itself to the business which is required of it. The day of trial does not come till the arrival of one of those seasons of commercial derangement known as monetary crises, when accidental and unforeseen causes defeat the reckonings and disappoint the expectations of mercantile men. It is, I conceive, in its power of meeting an occasion of this kind—in its capacity of expanding and contracting or maintaining its level, according to circumstances, and in such a manner as, while it secures the country against any depreciation from the standard, yet effects this end with the minimum of fluctuation in exchange value, and with the least disturbance to the general machinery of commerce—that its excellence as a monetary system consists. Now granting for the present, that the regulations of the Act of 1844 are adequate to secure the convertibility of bank notes, and thus to prevent their depreciation from the standard, there remains the further question, How far are they fitted for accomplishing the other end of a good system— the preservation of, as nearly as may be, a uniformity of value in the circulating medium under such sudden and violent oscillations as at times occur in the movements of the commercial world ?

The value of a circulating medium, convertible on demand into gold, of course depends in the long run on the cost of obtaining gold; but its value at any given time, and the fluctuations in its value, are determined by the quantity which happens to be in circulation, compared with the functions which it has to perform, and its efficiency in performing them:—that is to say, the value of a circulating medium depends on three distinct conditions ; the quantity of it in circulation ; the number of exchanges which it has to accomplish ; and its efficiency, or, as it is called in technical language, " the rapidity of circulation." Now, it is over one of these circumstances only that we can exercise directly any control. The number of exchanges to be performed depends upon the state of commerce in the country ; the rapidity of the circulation depends on the commercial facilities at the disposal of the public, the state of public confidence, &c. ; the only condition that we can control is the quantity, and this, in a mixed circulation like ours, is done by regulating the issue of bank notes. If, therefore, it be desirable that the currency be maintained as nearly as possible at a uniform value, the regulation of the issue of paper money should be made with constant reference to the other two conditions upon which its value depends,—that is to say, the number of exchanges taking place, and the rapidity of circulation ; providing, on the one hand, against any sudden reduction in the amount of notes issued, so long as the *bona fide* transactions to be performed remain undiminished, and on the other, furnishing some mode, on the occurrence of any sudden alteration either in the state of trade or in the state of public confidence, of compensating for this change by means of a corresponding contraction or expansion, as the case may be, in the quantity of notes issued. The principles here indicated are, I believe, generally recognized. Mr. M'Culloch, for example, (a strong supporter, by the way, of the Bank Charter Act) thus expresses himself:—* " The demand for money," he says, " differs at different periods. A currency susceptible neither of increase or diminution might be at one time in excess, and at another deficient, according to the varying state of credit and confidence in the country, and the nature of its commercial relation with foreigners. It is therefore of importance to bear in mind, that it is not by the absolute amount of currency that any correct judgment can be formed whether it be in excess or not. At one time, an issue of eighteen millions of Bank of England notes might be probably too great and under other circumstances an issue of twenty millions or twenty-five millions might not be enough."

Such being the conditions on which the value of a currency depends, and looking to the uncertain and fluctuating character of our transactions with foreign countries, as well as to the numerous circumstances which may affect credit and confidence at home, it appears to me that any system which, like the act of 1844, takes no account of these varying circumstances, but substitutes an inflexible rule for discretionary adjustment, and subjects the control of the paper issue to regulations prescribed without reference to what may be the state of trade or of public confi-

---

* M'Culloch's *Smith's Wealth of Nations*, note, p. 493.

dence in particular emergencies, labours under an inherent defect, and is calculated in periods of commercial derangement to intensify every cause of disturbance, and to convert pressure into panic.

The causes which may lead to a monetary crisis are various: over-trading beyond what the requirements of society may justify ; a speculative mania, leading to an imprudent extension of credit ; these bring in their train commercial disturbance, loss, and bankruptcy.   With regard to the influence which the issue of paper-money may exercise upon monetary crises arising from such causes, I am disposed to think the notions commonly entertained are greatly exaggerated. The history of the several crises which have occurred within the last sixty years goes to show that an increased paper circulation is the consequence, not the cause, of extravagant speculation and high prices ; and the remedy for such evils is, I conceive, to be found in a greater extension of free trade principles, and in whatever else conduces to greater certainty and stability in the character of commercial transactions, rather than in currency regulations. But, whatever may be thought upon this point, it is at least certain that the facilities supplied by the Bank of England to imprudent speculation have been greater since the passing of the Bank Charter Act, than were ever afforded previous to its enactment.   There cannot be a better measure of the facilities afforded to the public in this respect than the rate of interest.   Now, before the passing of the Bank Charter Act, in times of the greatest speculative excitement, as for example, in the year 1825, the Bank never lowered its rate of interest below 4 per cent. ; on the contrary, after the act had become law, the Bank reduced its rate of interest to 2 per cent. ; thereby undoubtedly encouraging, as far as undue banking accommodation was capable of encouraging, the numerous bubble schemes, principally railway projects of various kinds, which sprang up so exuberantly at that time, and by their absorption of the ordinary floating capital of the country added so considerably to the difficulties of the subsequent year. Indeed, this is one of the counts in the indictment which the Lords' Committee of 1848, in their report, bring against the conduct of the Bank of England.

It will not be necessary longer to dwell on monetary crises arising from causes of this kind ; it is sufficient for my purpose to point out that the Bank Charter Act has not opposed the slightest restraint to the speculative spirit in which they originate, but, on the contrary, is consistent with the most unbounded extension of it.

There are, however, other causes of commercial disturbance to which it will be necessary more particularly to advert, both because they are of a kind to which the present state of our relations with foreign countries renders us more immediately liable, and because they arise out of circumstances to which the regulations of the law of 1844 seem to be peculiarly inapplicable.

C

A monetary crisis may be occasioned not only by such incidents as have been alluded to—over-trading, and undue use of credit by merchants and other speculative persons—but also by circumstances which are in their nature quite unavoidable, or at least which can only be avoided at the expense of evils still more formidable than any extent of mere commercial loss. The country, for example, may be called upon to support large military expenditure abroad; or to pay for large additional imports of food; or other occurrences of a like character may happen; or several of these may concur. Now, in such cases, if the extent of our payments to foreign countries should exceed what our ordinary exports can at the moment discharge, a necessity will arise for remitting the balance in gold; and, if this balance be considerable, the consequence will be a severe pressure upon the money market, resulting, perhaps, in a monetary crisis.

This is a source of commercial derangement which the political condition of Europe at present gives us too much reason to apprehend, more particularly if anything like a short harvest at home should happen to coincide with a drain upon our resources, occasioned by extraordinary foreign military expenditure. It is, therefore, of importance to show what provision Sir Robert Peel's Act makes for meeting such a contingency.

The provisions of the act are, that £14,000,000 of notes only are to be issued on securities; the amount issued beyond that sum depending upon the amount of gold in the coffers of the bank. It consequently follows that, in the event of its being necessary to export gold to meet demands for foreign payments, the act would require that an equal amount of notes should be struck off the circulation ; that is to say, that if ten millions of gold be sent abroad to pay for necessary expenses, ten millions of notes also should be cancelled. Now, it is to be observed, that while this large quantity of gold is being exported to foreign countries, there would be nothing unwarrantable in supposing that all the other monetary transactions of the community might be going on as usual, or nearly so. The gold exported, having been before lying inactive in the cellars of the bank, was not operating as productive capital ; even if it should be considered as so much abstracted from the effective capital of the country, yet a deduction of ten millions from the currency of the country, is far more than an equivalent proportion to the same sum deducted from the capital of the country. Supposing, for example, that the total capital of the country was five hundred millions, and the currency fifty millions (the disparity between them being, in fact, probably much greater), ten millions deducted from each would reduce the capital of the country but two per cent., while it would reduce the currency twenty per cent. It is evident, therefore, that whether we consider the ten millions of gold which, by the hypothesis, is sent abroad to pay foreign debts, to be a deduction from the effective capital of the country or not, a contraction of the currency to the same extent is a contraction altogether disproportioned to whatever diminution such export of gold may be supposed to occasion in the legitimate bona fide dealings transacted at home. There is, in fact, nothing in the mere circumstance of the transmission of gold from the cellars of the Bank of England to foreign countries—considered in itself, and apart from artificial regulations—to interfere materially with the ordinary routine of commercial proceedings. Productive capital may still seek its accustomed channels ; industry pursue its wonted task ; consumption may proceed unchecked, or, if checked at all, only in proportion to the advance in prices ; in a word, while these large additions are being made to the foreign payments of the nation, the functions which the currency has to perform at home may continue without serious abatement.

It thus appears that, in the event of the occurrence of such contingencies as we have been considering,— large military expenditure in foreign countries, unusual importations of food to supply the defects of a short harvest, and other circumstances of a similar description,—while all the ordinary internal exchanges of the country may be proceeding without material alteration, the circulating medium in which these exchanges are to be transacted would, by the act of 1844, be subjected to a sudden and extraordinary contraction. It is further to be remembered that, in such times as we are supposing—times of pressure upon the money market—the confidence of mercantile men in the stability of those with whom they do business, is never so implicit as when trade is in its normal state. Tradesmen in such times cease to give their usual credit, and consequently the reduced circulation would have increased functions to perform ; both circumstances acting in the same direction, and tending greatly, according to the principles which have been already laid down, to enhance its value.

Now, when we consider the vast number of routine payments regularly transacted in London alone, absorbing, as I believe they do, a large proportion of the whole Bank of England circulation ; when we consider their imperative character, and the consequences of the slightest failure in a single engagement, it must be plain that a sudden and extensive reduction in the means of making these payments,—a sudden and unlooked-for enhancement in the value of the medium in which these engagements are to be discharged,— must lead to violent convulsions in what may be considered the heart of our monetary system. And when we further bear in mind the numerous ramifications of commercial relations throughout the country, and the intimate connexion between each and the centre of the circulation, it must be equally evident that any serious disturbance originating in the metropolis cannot fail to extend itself, and to produce grave and disastrous consequences amongst the general community.

It is no doubt an evil that the country should be

obliged to send abroad valuable things of any sort to meet, for example, the necessary expenses of war, for which it receives no return, at least no material return. This, however, is inevitable from the very nature of war, which means destruction and not production. But it seems a great and needless aggravation of this evil, that the law should be such as to render it impossible to discharge this necessary debt, without at the same time subjecting the circulating medium at home to such an extraordinary and gratuitous contraction, as must convulse the whole commercial community, and derange the entire machinery of our monetary system.

But it may be said, and this is the view of those who dictated the act of 1844, that, granting the reality of the evils adverted to, (for they cannot be denied) yet this is the price we must pay for securing the convertibility of our notes. " If you allow a certain amount of treasure," says Mr. Norman,* " to leave the Bank without any contraction, that treasure would become a part of the currency of other nations, and it will there remain ; there is no reason why it should come back at all ; *it never can come back unless a contraction really takes place.* Assuming it to be the case that it never comes back, in the course of a few years you have another drain, and if the vacuum is again supplied by the issues of paper here, that gold will not

---

* See his evidence before Select Committee on Banks of Issue, 1840, Q. 2177.

come back ; so that, upon that principle, there is no conceivable amount of reserve which you might not part with." " Unless contraction of the paper money," says Mr. Lloyd,* "corresponding to the drain upon the bullion, be resorted to, there can be no security in any course of action, and for this obvious reason: if the paper currency of this country be suffered to be depreciated in reference to the value of the currencies of other countries, even to a very slight extent, and if that depreciation be perpetuated by constantly keeping the amount of paper notes undiminished, upon that supposition, an amount of gold equal to the whole paper circulation, or even exceeding it, may be drained out." " Bullion," says Mr. M'Culloch,† "like other commodities, is exported only when its exportation is profitable. The fact that the exchange has fallen, and that bullion is being exported, proves incontestably that the currency is redundant ; and that, consequently, the directors of the Bank of England should immediately set about contracting their issues to prevent the exhaustion of their coffers."

These are the views which suggested the regulations of the Bank Charter Act ; and if they correctly represented all the causes which regulate the efflux and influx of the precious metals, the arguments which I have quoted would, to any one who regarded the convertibility of bank notes as a condition of primary importance, be decisive in favour of that Act.

---

* Evidence before Select Committee on Banks of Issue, 1840, Q. 2716.

† M'Culloch's *Smith's Wealth of Nations*, notes, p. 494, edit. 1850.

But I think it may be doubted if all the essential circumstances affecting the distribution of the precious metals are here taken into account. It is of course necessary to speak with great caution on a question on which some high authorities have expressed an opinion different from mine ; but if the matter were to be determined by an appeal to eminent names, the preponderance of authority would, I conceive, be still in favour of the view advocated in these pages. As this is a question, however, to be decided by an appeal to facts and principles rather than to names, instead of confronting the passages I have quoted with other passages of a contrary tendency from authorities of equally high standing (as I might easily do)* I shall venture, though with considerable diffi-

---

* For example, Mr. Tooke, the author of the History of Prices, in his examination before the Committee on Banks of Issue, 1840, is asked by Mr. Grote, Q. 3743 : " Are you of opinion that a mixed circulation of paper and coin ought to fluctuate in amount in the same manner and proportion as a metallic currency, if we had a metallic currency, would fluctuate ?—I am not at all clear that in a mixed circulation of coin and paper, it is desirable that the fluctuations in the amount should vary exactly with the fluctuations in the amount of bullion ; on the contrary, I believe that a variation in the amount of the circulation, corresponding exactly, or as nearly as might be, with the variation in the amount of bullion, would be exceedingly inconvenient, and occasion frequent and sometimes violent oscillations in the rate of interest, or, as it is technically called, the money-market.

"3744. If the paper circulation is to be preserved constantly conformable in value to gold, must it not conform in quantity constantly also to gold?—Not at all ; as long as the paper is strictly convertible into gold, it cannot be said that the value of the currency is impaired ; there may be a very considerable occasional demand for the export of the precious metals, without any ground of inference that the originating cause of it has been any excess of the circulation of this country : with a sufficient reserve of bullion on the part of the bank, *the probability is, that the gold would in such case return, and that there*

dence, to examine the question upon independent grounds.

And first I shall refer to a matter of fact. Mr. Norman says that gold, in the event of a foreign drain, " *can never come back, unless a contraction of the currency really take place.*" The answer to which assertion is, that during the last war the experiment was frequently tried, and the gold in every instance did come back, not only without any contraction having taken place, but even while the circulation was undergoing a considerable enlargement.

In Mr. Tooke's History of Prices (vol. 1, p. 157,) he remarks upon a circumstance to which he invites especial attention, the circumstance, namely, "that,

---

may have been no intermediate disturbance of that amount of the circulation, which was previously not in excess as compared with the ordinary transactions of the country.

"3745. Do not you think that, however large the reserve of gold in the hands of the bank might be at the period when the foreign drain began, if the bank were either to increase the quantity of bank notes in circulation, or even to decline contracting them during the course of the drain, the probability is very much increased indeed of the drain continuing to such an extent as to exhaust the bank reserve of bullion, and thus to frustrate the possibility of maintaining the convertibility of bank notes?—I believe that, with a large reserve of bullion at the commencement of any drain, if the bank simply kept their securities from increasing beyond the amount which, previously to the drain, they found that they had been able to preserve, without any obvious effect in causing an extreme depression of the rate of interest, they might retain that amount of securities, and then consequently, in all probability, there would be no material alteration of the circulation ; the bank might allow, to some extent, the drain to proceed without any forced operation, beyond a very moderate rise in the rate of interest. *I can conceive of hardly any circumstances which would not enable it, always supposing a large average reserve, to maintain very nearly the same amount of circulation, except in as far as it might be acted upon by the public, consistently with admitting of a reflux of bullion.*"

while the amount of bank issues was, from 1797 to 1817, undergoing, with trifling exceptions, a progressive increase, *the exchanges, upon every pause from the pressure of extraordinary foreign payments, tended to a . recovery;* and when the pressure had entirely ceased, the exchanges and the price of gold were restored to par, while the bank circulation was larger in amount that at any preceding period." So much for the general fact as given on the authority of Mr. Tooke. Referring now, for the sake of particular illustration, to the returns of the Bank of England circulation, bullion, &c. as given in the Appendix to the Report from the Committee on the Bank of England Charter, 1833, and looking to these returns from the year 1808 to the year 1817, during which interval the largest foreign war expenditure ever undertaken by this country took place, I find that the circulation

In Aug. 1808, amounted to	£17,111,290,	bullion	£6,015,940
In Aug. 1809, ,,	19,575,180,	,,	3,652,480
In Aug. 1810, ,,	24,793,990,	,,	3,191,850
In Aug. 1811, ,,	23,286,850,	,,	3,243,300
In Aug. 1812, ,,	23,026,880,	,,	3,099,270
In Aug. 1813, ,,	24,828,120,	,,	2,712,270
In Aug. 1814, ,,	28,368,290,	,,	2,097,680
In Aug. 1815, ,,	27,248,620,	,,	3,409,040
In Aug. 1816, ,,	26,758,720,	,,	7,562,780
In Aug. 1817, ,,	29,543,780,	,,	11,668,260

Thus it appears that the circulation, which in August, 1808, stood at the sum of about 17 millions, rose by tolerably regular steps, till in the August of 1817 it reached the amount of nearly 30 millions; while during the same period the bullion in the

Bank, which, under the action of foreign payments, fell at one time (August, 1814) so low as nearly to £2,000,000, yet in spite of a constantly increasing circulation, completely recovered from this foreign drain ; so that in the year 1817, when the notes in circulation amounted to nearly £30,000,000, the bullion in the Bank had reached 11,500,000 ; these sums being, respectively, the maximum amounts which the circulation and bullion had ever reached up to that time.   It is indeed somewhat remarkable that it was just at this time, when after a rapid increase of paper issue, the circulation had just attained its maximum, that the market price of gold, after its long aberrations from this standard, fell almost to par ; while the treasure in the Bank had at the same time become so abundant, that about this time, (in the months of April and September, 1817) the Bank Directors undertook by public notice to pay, and actually did pay, a large proportion of their notes in coin, amounting, it has been estimated, to about £5,000,000.*

A further negative to the doctrine laid down so peremptorily by Mr. Norman and Mr. Lloyd, is afforded by the state of the treasure and circulation respectively of the Bank of France between 1845 and 1847.   The figures which I am about to quote are taken from a return handed in by Mr. Tooke to the House of Commons Committee on Commercial Distress, 1848 (p. 422-3).

* See Tooke's History of Prices, vol. 2, p. 51, note.

Quarter ended	Circulation	Coin and bullion.
25th Mar. 1845,	... 256,000,000 francs	... 266,000,000 francs.
26th Dec. 1845,	... 269,000,000 francs	... 187,334,000 francs.
26th Dec. 1846,	... 259,459,000 francs	... 72,734,000 francs.
25th Mar. 1847,	... 249,404,000 francs	... 79,535,000 francs.

The Bank of France thus, between March, 1845, and March, 1847, parted with bullion to the amount of in round numbers 193,000,000 francs, or £7,500,000, (just about the same sum as the Bank of England parted with during the same period) while the circulation underwent no reduction worth speaking of. The rate of interest, too, was only raised from 4 to 5 per cent. Nevertheless, under these circumstances, the foreign drain was satisfied, and the gold returned.

These two examples from the history of the national banks of England and France, in two most important conjunctures, might, perhaps, be considered as furnishing a sufficient reply to that school of financiers who assert the interminable nature of drains, and the necessity of a contraction of the circulation as an essential condition in order to secure the return of gold to the country. The doctrine, however, is of such fundamental importance in currency questions, that it may be desirable to examine it more fully and upon general grounds.

The question is, in fact, one as to the circumstances by which the distribution of the precious metals among the different nations of the world is governed. The doctrine laid down by Mr. Norman, Mr. Lloyd, and Mr. M'Culloch, refers the movements of the precious metals exclusively to the state of the currencies of countries having commercial relations with each other. This is not stated in terms, but the assertion that adverse exchanges invariably indicate a redundant currency, the assertion that gold when once exported can *only* be drawn back into the country by means of an action upon the circulation, evidently imply this doctrine.

Now it appears to me that this theory is quite incomplete ; that it attributes an altogether undue importance to the influence of the circulation upon the movements of the precious metals, and that it overlooks entirely the operation of other causes which are at least equally important in their bearing upon the phenomena.

It is admitted, I believe, on a hands, that the efflux and influx of gold are in all cases ultimately governed by the relation between our exports and imports ; it is, therefore, as operating upon this relation, stimulating exportation and checking importation, that the contraction of the circulation is insisted upon as an essential condition of the return of gold. The doctrine is, that a reduced circulation has the effect of lowering prices ; that low prices act as an inducement to merchants to export more freely, and to import more sparingly ; that foreigners thus become indebted to us, and that, in payment of their debts, the gold is brought back to the country.

My objection to this theory is that, though true as far as it goes, it is incomplete. It is true that the tendency of a reduced circulation is to lower prices ;

it is true that a fall in prices does, within certain limits, operate as a stimulus to exportation and a discouragement to importation ; but it is not true that the motives to importation and exportation depend upon prices alone ; and, should the fall in prices be very sudden and violent, I conceive its effect on the whole would be rather unfavourable than otherwise on the exportation of commodities.

Upon what, then, does the state of our exports and imports depend ? Doubtless, a most important condition is the state of prices in this as compared with other countries. But this plainly is not the only circumstance affecting the question. The quantity of foreign goods, the quantity of tea, coffee, sugar, tobacco, wine, and the like, which we import from foreign countries, does not depend solely upon the prices at which these commodities are to be purchased ; it depends quite as much on the means at the disposal of people in this country for the procurement of such articles. If there should be a bad season at home, or a deficient harvest, or if there were a failure in the raw materials of any of our staple manufactures ; in a word, if any circumstance should occur to render industry less profitable, or to diminish the general wealth of the country, the means at the disposal of the community for the purchase of foreign commodities would be curtailed. Without supposing any alteration in prices, therefore, the demand for such commodities would decline, and consequently the amount of our imports would fall off. And, con-

versely, if the opposite conditions should occur, if the
wealth of the country were to increase, we should
each on an average have more to spend ; a portion of
this increased wealth, without necessarily supposing
any fall in prices abroad, would go in extra demand
for foreign commodities; and our imports would consequently increase.   It thus seems plain that any
circumstance which has the effect of enriching or
impoverishing the community, must operate in aug-
menting or diminishing the amount of goods which
we import from abroad ; and what takes place here
will of course take place equally in foreign countries.
It follows, therefore, that the relation between our
exports and imports, and, by consequence, the influx
and efflux of gold, depends not only on the state of
prices here and abroad, but also on the means of
purchase which are at the command, respectively, of
home and foreign consumers.   It is quite conceivable,
therefore, without supposing any alteration in the
prices of commodities, and consequently without the
necessity of any contraction of the circulation,—it
is quite conceivable, that the relation between our
exports and imports may be altered, and consequently
the exchanges adjusted, simply in consequence of a
change having taken place in the comparative wealth
of this and other countries.   Now, such a change
takes places whenever any of the causes come into
operation which I have referred to,—for example,
when the harvest fails at home, or when the staple of
any of our manufactures is deficient, or when large

military expenditure is to be supported abroad ; in short, when any of the ordinary causes occur which require this country to export gold. The transference of so much gold from this country to foreign countries —though it need not interfere to any great extent with the proceedings of commerce at home—yet alters the disposable wealth comparatively of this and other countries ; their means of expenditure is proportionally altered, and consequently their demand for each other's goods. There is thus, in the circumstances attending a transmission of gold from this country, a provision made for its return, quite independently of the state of prices, or of the circulation ; and this, I conceive, is the explanation of the phenomenon noticed by Mr. Tooke, and to which I have already referred, that during the war, notwithstanding a progressive increase in paper money, the exchanges under every pause from the pressure of foreign payments, tended to a recovery.

In attempting to prove, however, that the exchanges may adjust themselves otherwise than through the machinery of prices, and actually have so adjusted themselves, I by no means mean to deny that a low range of prices, co-operating with the other causes I have adverted to, may not hasten very much the desired re-adjustment, and therefore that some contraction of the currency on the occurrence of a drain for gold may not be a useful means of checking the drain and turning the exchanges in our favour, and therefore a proper measure to be adopted. But what

I do deny is, that a contraction of the circulation—
though a useful resource in connexion with other
causes—is by any means the sole or even an essential
condition for effecting that object, much less such a
contraction of the circulation as the act of 1844
enjoins—a contraction to the extent of the amount
of gold that is sent abroad. On the contrary, I conceive that so sudden and violent a contraction, while
it certainly will have the effect of lowering prices,
will also produce other effects, which in their tendency
are calculated to defeat the object the act has in view.

For, consider the full consequences of a sudden
and extensive fall in prices. A fall in prices would
undoubtedly, as has been admitted, be in the first
place an inducement to the merchant to hasten the
export of his goods on hand—so far, it may be admitted that a contraction of the circulation has the
effect of encouraging exportation; but, on the other
hand, it would also be a motive to him for abstaining
from giving his usual orders to the manufacturer.
The manufacturer, therefore, if he continued his productive operations, would be obliged to hold a larger
stock on hand, which would require him to become a
larger borrower than usual. But, in such a state of
the money market as we are supposing,—as the Bank
Charter Act would produce,—he could only extend
his loans by paying such a rate of interest as would
nearly absorb all his profits. It is further to be considered, that wages under the circumstances would
not fall in the same proportion as the prices of com-

D

modities would fall ; for it is well known that in
fluctuations of prices wages are always the last either
to rise or fall. The effect, therefore, of all these cir
cumstances—a falling off in orders, a very high rate
of interest, wages comparatively (in relation to the
price of commodities) high, would inevitably act as a
great discouragement to the fabrication of manufac
tures. The consequences to be expected in a greater
or less degree would be the closing of mills and work
shops, the turning off of hands, the general prostra
tion of productive industry. Now, not to mention
the injury which this state of things would inflic
upon the labouring classes, it does seem to be a some
what paradoxical doctrine to say, that exportation i
to be most effectually promoted by a measure which
has the effect of discouraging or putting a stop to
home production ; that we shall best secure the
return of gold into the country, by retarding or pre
venting the fabrication of those manufactures which
constitute our only means of purchasing it.

But the mischievous effects of such a policy would
not stop here. In addition to the check given to
productive industry, this sudden contraction of the
currency would have the further effect of producing
a very general disorganization in commercial affairs
Notwithstanding the deficiency in the means of effect
ing payments, there may be, in the circumstances w
are supposing, no corresponding want of *bona fide*
capital in the country. While the premises of the
shopkeeper or factor are empty, the warehouse of th

manufacturer may be proportionately full ; what is wanting is, such an amount of circulating medium as shall furnish the means of transferring the goods from one to the other. " There cease, at such times," says Mr. Thornton, in his work on Paper Credit,* " to be that regularity and exactness in proportioning and adapting the supply to the consumption, and that despatch in bringing every article from the hands of the fabricator into actual use, which are some of the great means of rendering industry productive, and of adding to the general substance of a country. Every great and sudden check given to paper credit, not only operates as a check to industry, but leads also to much misapplication of it. Some diminution of the general property of the country must follow from this cause ; and, of course, a deduction also from that part of it which forms the stock for exportation. It cannot be necessary to repeat," he adds, ' that on the quantity of exported stock depends the quantity of gold imported from foreign countries." " It seems sufficiently clear," says the same writer, in another place,† " that any very sudden and violent reduction of bank notes must tend, by the convulsion to which it would lead, to prevent gold from coming into the country rather than to invite it, and thus to increase the danger to the Bank itself. . . It is indeed in every respect plain, that it must be important to maintain carefully the credit

---

* Thornton on Paper Credit, page 85 ; 1802.　　　† Ibid. page 87.

of the country at that time in particular, when its guineas are few and also leaving it ;—that is the time when our funds are necessarily low, when the most regular industry should by every means be promoted, and when there is most need of the aid both of our domestic and foreign credit ; and it belongs to the Bank of England in particular, to guard and to super-intend the interests of the country in this respect."

On the whole, then, I can find no grounds, either in the principles of political economy, or in the especial circumstances attending commercial derange-ments, for supposing that the restrictions imposed by the act of 1844 are at all necessary towards securing the convertibility of our paper circulation ; though I think I can see how they are in many respects calculated to defeat that end. And it is hard to see on what other ground the principle of the act can be defended. In the rule which it lays down for the regulation of the paper issue, the only thing it takes notice of is the numerical amount of the circulation ; but the numerical amount of the circulation is, as regards the commercial facilities afforded to the pub-lic, a criterion altogether fallacious. This is dis-tinctly laid down in the Report of the Bullion Com-mittee of 1810. " The mere numerical return," says that Report, " of the amount of bank notes in circulation, cannot be considered as at all deciding the question whether such paper is or is not excessive. · · · The effective currency of the country de-pends on the quickness of circulation and the number of exchanges performed in a given time, as well as upon its numerical amount ; and all the circumstances which have a tendency to quicken or retard the rate of circulation, render the same amount of circulation more or less adequate to the wants of trade." It is a mistake, therefore, to suppose that the same amounts of currency are at all times equivalents. For example, in the autumn of 1847, £20,800,000 of notes were quite insufficient to carry on the commerce of the country ; in the following spring, £18,000,000 were more than enough ; and this was not because the business to be done on the former occasion was greater than on the latter ; but because, during the panic which prevailed in the autumn of 1847, a large portion of the circulation was paralyzed ; the numerical amount of bank notes, therefore, had ceased to be a measure of the effective currency.

Again, the act makes no provision for those disturbing incidents already adverted to, which tend to increase our liabilities to foreign countries, and require for their discharge an export of gold. In such cases the currency is regulated not with reference to the functions which it has to perform, but with reference to a transaction quite independent of this—the transmission of gold to foreign countries. The effect of this arrangement is to cause a contraction in the circulation altogether disproportioned to the diminution which takes place in the substantial means of the country, and therefore in the legitimate exchanges arising out of them. Engagements which were contracted when the currency stood at its ordinary level come to be performed after it has been violently reduced. The consequence is a difficulty, amounting, perhaps, to an impossibility, of obtaining the means of discharging stipulated payments,—leading probably to a general convulsion. " There is at least one object," says Mr. Fullarton,* " which would be effectually accomplished by acting on this system. It would be perfectly calculated, I think, to ensure that no derangement of the exchange, or none at least subsisting in coincidence with anything like pressure on the money market, should ever be permitted to pass off without one of those crises, hitherto fortunately of rare occurrence, but of which the results, when they have occurred, have been so extensive and so deplorable."

Nor, in providing for the convertibility of the note, does the act take any notice of the circumstances under which a drain for gold may take place. These are various. A drain for gold may proceed from external or internal causes, for the purpose of exportation, or for the purpose of hoarding. There were examples of both kinds in the year 1847 ; the drain in April took place under adverse exchanges, and the gold was sent abroad ; the drain in October took place while the exchanges were favourable, and in this case the gold was hoarded ; in fact, the drain in the latter instance acted as much upon Bank of England notes as upon gold.

* Fullarton on the Regulation of Currencies, page 137.

But the Bank Act makes no distinction between all the various cases of monetary pressure which may occur, proceeding from causes so different and sometimes opposite, and requiring remedies proportionately varied: it looks to the numerical amount of notes, and to that alone. The requirements of commerce may increase or diminish ; the circulation may be sluggish or active ; confidence or panic may be prevalent ; the exchanges may be favourable or adverse ; it does not signify ; the act makes no invidious distinctions; it still prescribes its £14,000,000 of notes on securities, and beyond that has no other remedy but what has been called " the cast-iron principle of notes for gold and gold for notes."

Well, this "cast-iron principle," from which its authors expected so much, was brought to the test of experiment. The years 1846–47, charged with such formidable events, arrived. A concurrence of misfortunes conspired to cause a heavy drain of gold to foreign countries ; as fast as the treasure was sent abroad, the screw was tightened upon the currency at home ; the result was, that our monetary system underwent a series of shocks and dislocations, such as it had never before experienced, and from which it was at length only rescued by an abandonment of the principle of the act, through a direct violation of the law. "If the law," says Mr. Samuel Gurney, (a stout supporter of the act when it was passed), "if the law had failed only in one case, I should have been jealous of alteration ; but we have had three periods of crisis and great difficulty in our monetary system in the last twenty-five months, in each of which I am certain that the calamity and difficulty were materially aggravated by this act. If there had been only one case, I should have wished to try it a little longer ; but when we have had three successive cases, one after another, and in each case the difficulty has been materially aggravated by it, I come to the solid conclusion that the act must be relaxed."*   "I think," says Mr. Tooke, "that the whole of the shock to commercial credit in the latter part of September and the first twenty-three days of October, was mainly attributable to the operation of the act."†   "The Bank itself," says Mr. Horseley Palmer, "was placed in danger, and the commercial credit of the whole country nearly paralysed; both which would have been obviated, had the power of extension beyond £14,000,000 then existed on the part of the Bank."‡

A brief sketch of some of the most remarkable features in the history of that memorable period will at once demonstrate the justice of the opinions I have quoted, afford an illustration of the working of the act under the influence of disturbing causes, and will enable me at the same time to substantiate and exemplify some of the objections which I have already advanced against it.

---

* Report of Secret Committee (House of Lords) on Commercial Distress, 1848, p. xxviii.

† Secret Committee of the House of Commons on Commercial Distress, 1848.   Q. 5336.   ‡ Ibid. Q. 1945.

The causes which led to the disasters of that time are well known. There was the potato failure, requiring immense importations of food ; there was the cotton failure, entailing a very high price for the raw material of a staple manufacture ; there was some over-speculation in transactions connected with the East; and, to crown all, there was the railway mania, rapidly converting floating capital into fixed, and rendering it, for all the purposes of foreign exchange, as unavailable as if it had been sunk in the British Channel. In addition to the ordinary exports, £9,000,000 in gold was sent abroad in discharge of our foreign engagements ; entailing, of course, under the bill of 1844, a proportionate reduction in the amount of bank notes issued. The effect of this concurrence of disturbing causes, all coming into operation under "the cast-iron system" of 1844, was such as those who took part in it will not easily forget. If we turn to the columns of the *Times* newspaper of that period, there is scarcely a day in which one—often half-a-dozen—failures of houses of long standing and high character are not announced. In London alone, during the autumn of that year, thirty-three great commercial houses broke down, the aggregate amount for which they failed being upwards of eight millions sterling : then followed in rapid succession the failures of the Royal Bank of Liverpool, the Liverpool Banking Company, the North and South Wales Banking Company, several private country banks, and the Union Bank of Newcastle, followed by a heavy run on many others. " I have been thirty years in business," says Mr. Hodgson, director of the Liverpool Bank, " and I never witnessed the feeling of helplessness and hopelessness so strong as in the last year ; there were heavier losses in 1825, but I never saw a greater feeling of discouragement ; persons not knowing what they could depend upon in looking to distant operations."* "The distress and pressure," says Mr. Horseley Palmer, " were greater than ever I remember."† " People thought," says another witness, " that they were in an iron cage and could not get out of it, and that cage was the Act of 1844."‡

But the most striking circumstance connected with the crisis of 1847 was not the extent of the calamity —that, perhaps, was equalled on other occasions; the characteristic feature of that crisis was the absolute impossibility of obtaining, on any terms, for the performance of the most essential contracts, the currency which the law of the country recognized as legal tender. It was not that accommodation could not be obtained for speculative projects,—speculation had at this time long ceased, and prices had long fallen ; it was not that doubtful men, who had no good security to offer, were left to their fate ; the peculiarity of the case was, that no security however unquestionable, no wealth however substantial, was of any avail for

---

* Secret Committee (House of Commons,) on Commercial Distress, Q. 95.
† Report of Lords' Committee, page viii.   ‡ Ibid.

obtaining the currency essential for the discharge of the most inevitable engagements.

In the month of October a bill, bearing the best English names, Messrs. Hormsby, and endorsed by the Bank of France, having only three days to run, was refused discount at the branch Bank of England in Liverpool.* On another occasion, the possessors of £60,000 of silver were unable to obtain the least advance upon it; the bank being restrained from issuing on silver beyond the extent of one-fifth of their bullion; "they came to the bank to sell, and the bank refused to buy."† "The cry has been," says a newspaper-writer of that time,‡ "not so much the rate of interest, but the power to obtain money at all." "At that time," says Mr. Gurney "we had a circulating medium of £20,800,000, and yet there was great difficulty in knowing where to get £1000."§ A curious proof of the same fact—the dearth of legal currency at the time—is afforded by the following statement which I have extracted from the *Times* of October 22nd, 1847 ; it is from the letter of a special correspondent sent to Liverpool to report on the state of commercial affairs. "In regard especially to banking affairs," the writer observes, " we may notice a feature tending to the relief of the money market, namely, that, contrary to the letter of their contracts

---

* See Mr. Hodgson's evidence before Committee on Commercial Distress, (House of Commons), 1848, Q. 71.

† Speech of Mr. Thomas Baring (House of Commons), 10th May, 1847.

‡ *Manchester Guardian.*

§ Evidence before House of Commons on Commercial Distress, 1848, Q. 1737.

with the Bank of England, those banks in England which have accounts with the metropolitan establishment are now, and have been for some days, permitted to pay out bills of exchange as cash." It thus happened that that accommodation which the act of 1844 had prohibited, the extreme urgency of the case had driven parties to supply for themselves by a kind of evasion of the law ; and bills of exchange were fast beginning to perform the functions of bank notes.*
Another indication of the same peculiar feature in this crisis—a dearth of currency altogether disproportioned to the scarcity of real wealth—is to be found in the fact, that a considerable number of the houses which stopped payment were thoroughly solvent houses ; houses which afterwards paid 20s. in the pound, and which could, if necessary, as was stated by one of the witnesses before the House of

---

* The same fact—the partial substitution of bills of exchange for bank notes in discharge of engagements contracted to be paid in bank notes—is attested by Mr. Hodgson, in his evidence before the Secret Committee (House of Commons) on Commercial Distress, 1848, Q. 194-195. It is, perhaps, worth while remarking that Mr. Thornton, writing 46 years before this time, in his work on Paper Credit, when discussing the effects of such a sudden action upon the circulation as the act of 1844 afterwards prescribed, distinctly points out that the consequence adverted to would ensue. The passage is as follows :—
" The case which has been put is, however, merely hypothetical ; for there is too strong and evident an interest in every quarter to maintain, in some way or other, the regular course of London payments, to make it probable that this scene of confusion should occur ; or, even if it should arise, that it would continue. Whether there might chance to be much or little gold in the country, *steps would be taken to induce the Bank to issue its usual quantity of paper, or measures would be resorted to for providing by some means a substitute for it.*" (Edition, 1802 ; page 76.) This is an accurate prediction of what actually did happen in the year 1847.

Commons' Committee, have as easily paid 40s. or 60s. in the pound.

Now, making all allowance for the operation of those circumstances already indicated, in which the difficulties of that time originated—the immense importations of food, the high price of raw cotton, the numerous railway and other bubble schemes— making all due allowance for the destruction and abstraction of capital and the disorganization of trade which such agencies were calculated to effect ; there is yet, I maintain, in the facts which have been adduced what none of these circumstances, nor all of them combined, can adequately account for.   All the damage that such agencies can be fairly charged with must be such as can be resolved into a loss of *bona fide* property of one kind or other ; but they fail entirely to explain why a man with £60,000 of silver could obtain no advance upon it in legal currency ; they do not explain why firms were obliged to stop payment, whose assets a month afterwards more than doubled their liabilities ; they fail wholly to explain the substitution of bills for bank-notes, contrary to the terms of contracts. These and other analogous phenomena are such as can only be accounted for by reference to the state of our currency laws.   But neither, it is to be remarked, will the solution of the problem be found in the small numerical amount of bank-notes in the hands of the public The numerical amount of the circulation was, at the time of greatest pressure, but little if at all below

the average (a proof, by the way, how fallacious a
criterion this affords as to our monetary condition).
The evil lay not in the gross amount of the currency
being inadequate, but in its *effective* amount being
inadequate.   It is estimated by Mr. Gurney, that of the
£21,000,000 of Bank of England notes in the hands
of the public, between £4,000,000 and £5,000,000
were lying inactive in the hands of private bankers,
for all the purposes of currency quite inoperative.
There was capital in the country ; there was currency
in the country ; but neither could be got to perform
its functions ; the system was paralyzed by univer-
sal distrust.   Now this distrust can, I conceive, be
shown distinctly and solely to be traceable to the
restrictive provisions of the Act of 1844.

To appreciate the operation of the Act in producing
the effects attributed to it, it is necessary to advert to
the state of the reserve in the banking department of
the Bank of England, during the period of extreme
pressure in October, 1847. This reserve is the sole fund
at the disposal of the bank for the public accommodation.   In healthy times, it fluctuates between about
£7,000,000 and £10,000,000.   Under the influence
of the several exhausting causes pressing during that
year on the resources of the bank—aided also by in-
judicious conduct on the part of the bank directors—the
reserve had been brought down to about £2,000,000 ;
the portion of it in the central establishment in London did not much exceed £1,500,000. This fund, far
from being sufficient to afford anything like the ordi-

nary accommodation to the public, was scarcely adequate to meet the demands of depositors; and there
was no means of recruiting it. The only two possible
means by which it could have been recruited were by a
sale of securities, or by an increased issue of notes ;
but the former resource the state of the money market
rendered impracticable,* the latter the act of 1844
interdicted. The bank, therefore, had come to the
end of its resources, and, so long as the restrictive
law continued, was incapable of giving accommodation upon *any* terms. Here, then, was the efficient
cause of the panic and of the evils which resulted from
it. Country bankers, before making their usual advances to their customers, naturally took the precaution of
ascertaining if they could count upon their ordinary
accommodation from the Bank of England ; but the
Bank of England was tied in the meshes of the
Charter Act, and could promise no discounts upon
any terms ; the securities offered might be unquestionable, there might be no objection to the rate of
interest, but the funds of the bank had run dry and
could not be recruited. The country banks, therefore, having no prospect of their ordinary accommodation, naturally increased their reserves of notes,
and refused to their customers the usual advances.
The feeling was thus propagated from banks to companies, from companies to individuals.   Every one

---

* See Mr. Tooke's evidence, House of Commons' Committee on Commercial
Distress, 1848.   Q. 5472–5 ; also Mr. H. Palmer's evidence before House of
Lords' Committee, 1848, p. xv. Report.

who had engagements to meet was thrown on the defensive ; he clutched closely whatever portion of the coin of the realm happened to come into his hands, and awaited the result.   Nor was the panic an unreasonable or unreasoning one.   True, the currency in the hands of the public was sufficient for their purposes if people had only trusted each other ; but this, though proved by the event, no one knew at the time.   All that was known was, that no man could reckon on the means of obtaining his usual accommodation upon any terms ; and, under these circumstances, to have failed to provide adequately against contingencies which could not be calculated upon, instead of being a proof of philosophic sagacity, would have been nothing else than foolhardy recklessness.

While things stood thus, the letter of the Government suspending the Act appeared, and the panic was instantaneously allayed.   The rock had been struck, and forthwith the currency gushed out from the hoards where it had been accumulating, and in the course of a week became so abundant, that the difficulty was no longer how to get money, but how to dispose of it.*   And why was this ?   Was it, as some

---

* Mr. Samuel Gurney, in his examination before the Secret Committee (House of Commons), on commercial distress, 1848, gave an account of an incident that occurred to his own firm, and which, as putting in a striking point of view the effect of the issue of the government letter, may be worth quoting here.   He is asked (Q. 1599),

" What was the effect of the issue of the government letter ?—The effect was that of immediate relief : perhaps I cannot explain the case better than by telling

have contended that the Government letter, destitute of any real efficacy, acted with a kind of talismanic influence on the imaginations of the people—with a

---

the history of my own firm on the day on which the government letter came down, and the previous Saturday : up to that Saturday our firm had no occasion to apply for any assistance from the Bank of England ; in consequence of the feeling of panic we had on the Saturday to get possession of the circulating medium, I went over to the governor of the Bank to negotiate an advance ; I was received by him, as I have always been in that establishment, with great courtesy, but I was told that they could not give me an answer till two o'clock in the day, but that they would, if practicable, make a point of letting me have the money. They gave me a pretty strong expectation that they would, but that they should charge me ten per cent. interest.

" Have you any objection to mention the amount ?—The amount was £200,000; whether £20,000 more or less I cannot say. I stated to the governor that it was a matter perfectly immaterial whether we lost two, or three, or four hundred pounds in such a transaction, but that I thought it would have a very injurious effect if it were stated in the city that our firm had paid ten per cent. I strongly urged this, and he was kind enough to relax to nine per cent., but below that he was quite unwilling to go, and we paid nine per cent. That was on Saturday. On the Monday morning there was the same cloud over the city ; there was a strong desire, both on the part of gentlemen from the country and bankers in London, to get possession of circulating medium, as they most reasonably thought, while it was to be had ; and a very great variety of orders came in from the bankers for sums of money, and from others not bankers. I went over to the Bank (or my partner), and stated that we should want a similar sum ; we were received with the same courtesy, and told that at two o'clock they would let us know whether we could have it or not ; before two o'clock this relaxing letter had come down, and very generally the orders for money were withdrawn ; they said, " we do not want the money now—we do not want the money now—there is no occasion to pay it." Sums of money were immediately offered us, and people then began to have confidence to use the notes which they had. *Before the week was over, we had to go and ask the Bank, as a favour, to let us repay the money which we had borrowed.*

" Are you of opinion that if the government letter had been issued earlier, any part of the pressure would have been saved ?—I have no hesitation whatever in saying that the severity and the extent of the calamity would have been limited had that letter come at an earlier period."

In short, if the case against the Act, in its influence upon the transactions of 1847, be not decisive, it is difficult to conceive what amount of evidence could

E

sort of ' Open, Sesame !' power upon the tills of bankers ?   Nothing of the kind.   That letter, announcing the suspension of the Act, was merely an obvious remedy working its natural and inevitable effect, the effect which   all whose eyes were not   blinded by their theories foresaw, and predicted it would produce.   It enabled the Bank of England to say to their customers, what the Act of 1844 had prevented them from saying, viz.:—" We can undertake to promise you accommodation at 8 per cent. if you require it." The moment this accommodation could be calculated upon, the necessity for hoarding had ceased.   The coun-

---

make it so. We have, first, the body of evidence put forward in the text, showing that, after allowing for the effects of all other causes, there was a residual calamity which nothing but the state of our currency laws was adequate to account for. We have then a number of deputations from the first mercantile bodies in the kingdom, waiting upon government, pointing to the restrictive clause of the act as the place where the shoe pinched, and urging its suspension. We have then the experiment actually tried, and with the most complete success. We have the necessity of the suspension strongly asserted in the unanimous verdict of two secret committees of the two Houses of Parliament, and admitted even by the authors of the act. We have one of those committees passing a sweeping censure upon the act, and charging it with a large portion of the evils of the crisis. We have the other committee, composed chiefly of the framers and abettors of this law, while it exonerates the act by a narrow majority of two (thirteen to eleven) from the same sweeping censure, yet, with more truth than logic, approving of its suspension, and admitting that it is unfit to meet the case of severe commercial pressure. Yet, in the face of this evidence, we still hear it roundly asserted that the effect of the act was greatly to ' mitigate' the commercial evils of that year ; that in fact the operation of the measure was peculiarly happy and beneficent, the cry for monetary accommodation a delusion, and the issue of the government letter a superfluous impertinence (see McCulloch's *Smith's Wealth of Nations*, 1850, p. 507.) " Five minutes before Moses struck the rock," says Sydney Smith, " there are men who would deny that the people were thirsty." We see the same denial may be made after the water has gushed out, and the people have drunk their fill.

try banks freely distributed their large reserves ; the
circulation flowed down into its natural channels ;
and, though not a note was issued by the Bank beyond
the limit set by the Act, the mere consciousness on
the part of the public that, if necessary, notes might
be issued, the knowledge that a discretionary power
had taken the place of an inflexible rule, was sufficient to restore confidence, and to render the circulation adequate to all the wants of the community.

But the full extent of the danger in which this
restrictive law involved the country has yet to be
stated. The Bank itself was placed in imminent
jeopardy. While its reserve in London had been reduced to £1,500,000, the deposits of the London
bankers alone considerably exceeded that sum.*
These deposits might have been called for at any
moment ; any accident might have led to a demand
for them. Now, had these deposits been called for,
the Bank of England must have stopped payment ;
and had this occurred, its notes would have ceased to
be legal tender. The effect would have been, that all
that portion of the reserve of country banks which
consisted of Bank of England notes would, *as reserve*,
have come useless ; they could no longer have been
given in payment of country bank notes. Under
these circumstances, there would have been great
reason to fear that the whole of the Bank of England
notes held at this time by the country bankers, and

---

* See Mr. Tooke's evidence before Secret Committee (House of Commons)
on Commercial Distress, 1848. Q. 5477-8.

which amounted to about six millions,* would have been returned on the central establishment.   Had this taken place, it would nearly have exhausted the treasure in the issue department, which was at this time under £8,000,000 ; and the remaining £2,000,000 would almost certainly have been carried off in the general confusion and dismay which such a run would have inevitably occasioned.   In short, it is the opinion of several witnesses of great practical experience, examined before the committees of 1848, an opinion confirmed by the Report of the House of Lords' Committee, that nothing but the tardy inter-position of the Government saved the convertibility of the note, which the stringency of the Act had en-dangered.†

But while the Bank Charter Act was thus pro-ducing a pressure and panic of its own, altogether independent of the circumstances which had origi-nated these disastrous occurrences, was there any justification to be found for this otherwise gratuitous mischief, in the dangers which were then threatening the Bank ?   Was gold leaving the country in such

---

* See Mr. Hodgson's evidence before Secret Committee (House of Commons) on Commercial Distress, 1848. Q. 94.

† In the examination of Mr. Hodgson, confidential director of the Liverpool Bank, before the Secret Committee of the House of Commons on Commercial Distress, 1848, Q. 94, he is asked,—" With regard to securing the converti-bility of notes, what is your opinion of the bill ?—I do not think it has secured the convertibility of notes at all. The notes remained convertible up to the suspension of the bill ; but I believe that if the bill had not been suspended then, or some similar measure adopted, notes would have ceased to be converti-ble."

quantities as to cause alarm ? Was the bullion of the Bank so reduced as to justify this resort to extreme measures of restriction ? On the contrary, the exchanges had been for three months in our favour ; upwards of £2,000,000 of gold had come into the country between August and October ; and there were still £8,000,000 in the coffers of the Bank. But the gold which was coming into the country, instead of going, as in times of confidence it would, to the Bank of England, scared away from the iron cage which the Charter Act had provided for it, found its way to the tills of private traders, and, as circulation, became inoperative.

Or could it be said that the excessive severity of the pressure which the Act was occasioning, was tending ultimately to right the system, by its action upon our exports and imports ; and that thus compensation for the immediate mischief would be afforded, by the future adjustment which it tended to bring about ? Was the pressure, in a word, stimulating our exports and checking our imports, in conformity with the views of those who represent a contraction of the currency as the one and only means of adjusting the exchanges ? On the contrary, it was tending to exactly the opposite result, and thus affording a direct negative to those views. Its operation in this respect may be gathered from the address of the deputation of Liverpool merchants, who waited upon Government on the 18th Oct., 1847. This deputation was composed of Mr. W. Brown, M.P., Mr. Cardwell, M.P., Mr. Wilson,

Patten, M.P., the Mayor of Liverpool, Mr. Horsfall, and others. "At present," the address observes, "produce of every kind could only be disposed of at an enormous sacrifice. *Orders from abroad for goods or produce could not be executed, from the impossibility of converting into cash the bills drawn against them.*" The memorial then proceeds to advert to the necessity of a temporary advance by Government. "It would effect," they say, "an immense benefit for the mercantile classes, and, by tending to allay groundless alarms, cause the release of large sums of money, which are now locked up and comparatively profitless, in consequence of the panic which prevailed. The accounts daily received from the manufacturing districts inform us, that houses of the greatest respectability and most ample resources had bent before the overwhelming pressure of the present moment ; and those who were most experienced in monetary affairs agreed in saying, that if Government did not immediately come to the relief of bankers, merchants, and traders, on whose prosperity so much of the wealth of the country depended, the result would be that houses now solvent, and possessing ample means (if their securities were convertible into ready money) would be involved in the common ruin." Thus this excessive tightening of the money market, to which its authors looked as the sole means of stimulating exportation, and thus aiding the adjustment of the exchanges, was tending directly towards the opposite result. It was fast deranging all the operations of industry, and sapping those resources of returning wealth on which the country ultimately must rely for restoring its balance of trade, and thereby securing the metallic basis of its currency.

The same point is directly established by the testimony of witnesses of first-rate authority, before the committees of 1848. Mr. Hodgson,* in his examination before the House of Commons' Committee, is asked, " Can you give any opinion as to the effect upon the export trade of the great difficulty which existed in discounting?—For a time it almost suspended the export trade." " By the impossibility of getting discount ?—Yes, it has almost suspended the export trade, *and in that way retarded the adjustment of the exchanges.*" Before the same committee Mr. Samuel Gurney† is asked, " Did it come under your notice that the difficulty of obtaining discounts in April and October had any effect upon the export trade ?—A very decided effect in checking the export trade." Again he is asked, " In the imports of corn, when the profits may be 50 or 60 or 100 per cent., do you think that the raising the rate of interest would check a speculation of that kind ?—It would not." So that while the action of the Bank was powerless in restraining importation in times of speculative excitement, it had a very decided effect in checking exportation under monetary pressure.

* Evidence before Secret Committee, (House of Commons) 1848, Q. 287-8
† Evidence before same Committee, Q. 1934-6.

It is in this way that the Bank Charter Act operates in adjusting an adverse balance of trade.

It thus appears that this Act, as it fails to satisfy the conditions of a correct theory of currency, deduced from the nature of a circulating medium and the functions which it has to perform ; so also, when brought to the test of a commercial crisis—the test which may be considered as the *experimentum crucis* of a monetary system—it has proved a signal and complete failure.

During the memorable period which we have been considering, what one of the requisites of a good system can this law be said to have fulfilled ? What one of the objects for which it was enacted can it be said to have accomplished ? Did it place a restraint upon speculation in the earlier stages of confidence and excitement ? On the contrary, the public received from the Bank of England under the present charter an extent of banking facilities quite unprecedented. Did this law, when distrust had succeeded to confidence, enable the Bank to atone for the mischief it had stimulated, by coming forward with a judicious liberality to relieve the excessive pressure ? On the contrary, its restrictive provisions just became really operative when a full discretion was required, and thus the inevitable evils of the times were aggravated by a panic, the fruits solely of its Procrustean enactments.* It did not save from a suspension of pay-

---

* The following quotation is from the money article of the *Times*, Oct. 2nd, 1847, and, as coming from a well-informed and intelligent observer during the progress

ments the most solvent and prudent houses—houses of which the assets were more than double the liabilities. It did not preserve the money market from fluctuations in the rate of interest greater than till then had ever been heard of. It did not secure the Bank of England from the imminent danger of suspension. Even the convertibility of our paper circulation was, under the guardianship of this principle, placed in the utmost jeopardy, and only saved by discarding it. The law has proved itself wholly unfit to meet the strain of disturbing forces ; and this being so, it would seem important, now when we are entering upon a period more than usually liable to monetary derangements and difficulties of various kinds, that public attention should be drawn towards this subject, in order that our currency code, with which so much of the commercial prosperity of the country

---

of events,—from one also highly favourable to the present law,—is well deserving of attention. On recording the resolution of the Bank of England to discontinue advances on Stock and Exchequer Bills, the writer observes, " The natural results of the measure adopted by the Bank of England, on the 2nd September" (the lowering of the rate of interest one-half per cent.) " have taken place to-day, and the city has witnessed another panic consequent on the proceedings of that institution. Four weeks back, in the face of a steady decrease of their reserve of notes, notice was given that advances should be made on Stock, Exchequer Bills, &c., at five per cent., being a reduction of full one-half per cent. on the rate then current in the market. They now refuse advances on these securities on any terms. *The Bank is always the first in the field to add to the terrors of any existing crisis.*" On October 8th, 1847, the same writer remarks, " How long the public will continue to tolerate the accumulated injuries and disgraces which the Bank thus continues to inflict on the nation, it is needless to inquire ; but *it is right that the evils should be attributed to their true cause while they are in actual progress.*"

is bound up, and on which its ability to support the exhaustion of, it may be, a protracted war is so largely dependent, may have the benefits of such modifications and improvements, as those whose experience and opportunities entitle them to advise in such matters may suggest.

Without pretending to propound any definite scheme for the regulation of the currency, which must be left to those practically versed in banking affairs, I would venture to call attention to some general principles which apply to this subject, and which, in the copious discussions the question has at various times undergone, have already, with more or less cogency, been elicited.

There is a school of economists who oppose the principles of the Act of 1844 on grounds wholly distinct from those which have been advanced in the foregoing pages. I allude to those persons who advocate what is called " free-trade in banking." Such persons conceive that any interference on the part of the state in the transactions of private individuals, in which they may be supposed to be themselves the best judges of their own interests, is a proceeding at variance with the broad principles of free-trade ; and they hold, with respect to the issue of bank notes, as with respect to the production of all other commodities, that the best security for the public is to be found in the mutual competition of producers. If, it may be said, A can induce B to take his promises to pay on demand, in discount of a bill ; if B can induce C to receive those same promises to pay, in satisfaction of a debt ; and if the notes issued by A thus get into circulation, why, it may be asked, should the state interfere ?   Each of these parties may be supposed to know his own interest better than the state can know it ; no one need receive the notes if he does not please ; they are not legal tender ; and if these parties all find it their convenience to carry on their dealings in this way, why should they be hampered by restrictions, founded upon the exploded fallacy that the state understands the interests of its members better than the individual members them-selves ?

This, I believe, is the view of those who advocate free-trade in banking ; and it is, at least, sufficient to throw the onus of proof upon their opponents—to require those who would subject the issue of bank notes to legal restrictions, to make out, with respect to the currency, clear grounds for exceptional treatment— to show that the principles of free-trade and un-restricted competition are here inapplicable.   Now, without pretending to enter fully into this question, it will be enough for my purpose to show that the currency does constitute an exceptional case ; and that the reasons which, in the production of commodities generally, render free competition the best security for the public interest, do not obtain in the case of the issue of paper money.

Currency differs from all other commodities in this, that it is not only a commodity but a measure of value, and on this ground it is that coining is properly considered a prerogative of state. The privilege of coining has always been invested with a number of sanctions ; and the same reasons which apply to coining apply in a still stronger degree to the issue of paper money. A paper currency only answers its purpose so far as it takes the place of coin, and performs all that coin would perform. Inasmuch, therefore, as paper money thus becomes a measure of value, it belongs to the state to regulate it. But there is a further reason for state control in the case of paper money, that does not exist in the case of coin. Upon coin issued in the intrinsic metal there is no profit to be made ; when paper money is issued, as the paper is intrinsically worthless, there is a profit to the extent of the issue. Now, there is no reason why any individual should be permitted to monopolize this profit ; it is the property of the public, and should go to the state. This principle is recognized in those provisions of the Act of 1844 which require the Bank to pay, in services or otherwise, for its privilege of issuing £14,000,000 of notes without a metallic basis. The stamp duty upon bank notes is also of the same nature.

The principles of free-trade applied to the issue of notes would be inconsistent with the functions which notes are intended to perform. A bank note is not simply a piece of paper issued on the credit of the person who issues it, and who is obliged to pay it in the legal coin of the realm ; it is a substitute for coin, and is intended for the purpose of currency, which, by the very definition of the term, means that it should pass from hand to hand without question. But this purpose would be defeated if any man were permitted, without guarantee of any kind, to issue his notes payable on demand to any person who would take them. The exigencies of traders would at times give them no choice but to take such notes, which, thus getting surreptitiously into the genuinely-sound paper currency, would discredit the whole of it, and render it unfit to perform the offices of currency.

Lastly, the principle of unrestricted competition is inapplicable to the regulation of the currency. The advantages of competition in all ordinary cases depend upon these circumstances,—that the public are interested in obtaining the greatest quantity of the article produced at the cheapest price ; that the loss from over-production falls exclusively on the producer; and that it is the interest of the producer to conform to the proper rule by which the supply should be adjusted to the demand. Now, with regard to paper money, the object which competition secures is not that in securing which the public is most concern-ed. What the public requires is not the greatest quantity of currency at the cheapest price, but just such a quantity as shall circulate the commodities to be exchanged in the country, at a value corresponding to a given standard. Again, when over-production occurs in the case of paper money, the loss does not

fall exclusively or principally on the producer, but
chiefly on the public who hold his notes. Nor is it
the interest of the issuer of notes to regulate his issue
so as to keep their value exactly up to the standard ;
on the contrary, it is the interest of each separate
issuer to violate this rule. The issue of notes, therefore, should not properly be considered as a trade at
all, but as a state prerogative, for which, if delegated
to any body, the public should require an equivalent ;
and the nature of the currency, and the functions
which it has to perform, clearly take it out of the
class of cases to which the principles of free-trade and
the advantages of unrestricted competition apply.

The principle of competition being thus shown to
be unsuited to the regulation of the issue of paper
money, there would seem to be no advantage obtained
in permitting a plurality of issuers ; and, indeed, on
theoretical grounds, a single source of issue appears
to be altogether the most desirable arrangement. I
am unable, however, to see in this circumstance the
extreme importance that Mr. McCulloch and others
are disposed to attribute to it ; nor do I suppose that
the public advantages which would arise from restricting the privilege of issuing notes to a single
source, would be at all an equivalent for the hardships
which such a measure would inflict upon existing
private interests. In this respect, the course taken
by the Bank Charter Act, restricting the privilege of
issuing to such banks of issue as were established at
the time the act passed, and offering an inducement

to the abandonment of the privilege, was, perhaps, on the whole, a fair and judicious one.

The next point to be noticed is one which appears to me to be of fundamental importance, namely, that in the last resort the issue of notes, whether committed to one or more issuers, should be entrusted to the discretion of some man or body of men. No system of rules however ingeniously contrived can, so far as I can see, supersede the necessity of this. In the course of the foregoing observations, several arguments have been advanced in support of this position, showing that a fixed inflexible rule, laid down without reference to what may be the state of trade and of public feeling in particular conjunctures, is quite incompatible with the preservation of that uniformity of value in the circulating medium, which is one of the first requisites of a good system. I shall subjoin in the note the opinions of some of the highest practical and scientific authorities upon this point, given in their evidence before the parliamentary committees.*

---

* Mr. Hodgson is asked (Secret Committee of the House of Commons on Commercial distress, 1848, Q. 307), "You think the bank ought to exercise a discretion, and not to act upon general rules?—I do think so; in the first place, wherever circumstances affecting the state of credit are at all brought into circulation, they cannot go by general rules; they must take other considerations into account, and advert to the probable state of things; I cannot conceive of fixed and absolute rules being compatible with the intelligent administration of a bank, and still less with the management of the circulation." In another place (same Committee, Q. 373) he observes upon the same point, "Almost every difficulty we have to consider on this point drives us at last back to a better administration of the affairs of the Bank, because that administration cannot be mechanical: there must be discretion somewhere, and the point

It is true there will always be a certain amount of
risk and danger in any system which is confided to
the discretion of fallible men. The leaving anything
to discretion implies a corresponding degree of imper-
fection in the machine ; and there is doubtless something in the notion of a self-acting system that conduces to the serenity and self-glorification, perhaps, of
its framers. But those who are carried away by this
idea should remember that, under the Act of 1844,
while the hands of the bank are tied in times of pressure from giving effectual relief, the system is yet as
much as ever liable to all the perils that are inseparable
from discretionary power; it has, in fact, all the evils
which belong to a system resting on discretionary
power without its advantages. The great mischief to
be apprehended on this score is improvident liberality

---

to aim at is to secure as much discretion as we can in those to whom we con-
fide so important an office as the administration of the currency."

Mr. Horseley Palmer, approving of the limitation of the issue to £14,000,000
as a principle of management for ordinary times, yet considers that for emergencies there must be a power of relaxation. " Then you would leave it (he is
asked by the Secret Committee, 1848, Q. 1954-5) to the discretion of the
Bank to relax when they thought fit to do so ?—Yes, unless you saw fit to
place any control over the Bank in the hands of any member of Her Majesty's
Government."—"You would leave an unlimited discretion either in the Bank alone,
or in the Bank checked by a Government officer?—Yes." In Mr. Tooke's
examination he is asked (by the same Committee, Q. 5,392-3), " In all cases
the prudent management must depend upon the circumstances out of which the
drain arises ?—Yes, most unquestionably. You may try numberless experi-
ments, but you must at last come to that conclusion : there is no system of
banking that must not at last depend on prudent management." " Is it your
opinion, therefore, that a large discretion should be allowed to those who have
the management of such important institutions ?—Unquestionably," &c. He
then goes on more fully to develope his views. It would be easy to add to
these quotations, but the above will perhaps be sufficient.

on the part of the Bank at one time, obliging it at another, in self-defence, to resort to sudden action.* Now there is as much room for mismanagement in this respect under the present law, in dealing with the banking department, as under the former system, when the two departments were united and the regulation of the issue was left to the judgment of the directors. In each case, what they have to exercise their judgment upon is the treatment of their reserve: in one case this reserve is the amount of notes held by the banking department; in the other, it is the amount of treasure in the cellars of the Bank. When the directors become aware of the difficulties of their position, they have, in the latter case, a large margin to deal with, and their hands are free to act according to their sense of what the emergency requires. In the former, the margin is liable to be so reduced as naturally to excite alarm, while the knowledge on the part of the public that the Bank is bound within inflexible rules tends, as it happened in 1847, to convert the alarm into panic. Their action may in such cases be expected to be more sudden; its effects on the money market more violent; and consequently the dangers to be apprehended from a discretion, thus acting within narrow limits, more formidable than if it were entirely unshackled.

Again, if it should be thought that in thus advocating the necessity of a discretionary power for the

---

* See Mr. Lloyd's examination before Secret Committee (House of Commons) on Commercial Distress, 1848, where this point is fully admitted.

F

regulation of the issue, (subject of course to the obligation of paying in gold upon demand), we are claiming
for a paper currency that which could have no place if
the currency were metallic—since there would be no
such means of multiplying sovereigns at pleasure ; it
should be remembered that the analogy between a
metallic and paper currency can under no circumstances be complete.   There must always be this
broad distinction between them, that the medium
which in the one case possesses intrinsic value, is, in
the other case, intrinsically worthless.   Every one
who possesses a coin knows exactly what he can cal-
culate upon, and this quite independently of mint
regulations ; but under a paper currency, the value of
the note being wholly conventional, to satisfy the
holder of the note of its value there is need of public
confidence.   Now the maintenance of this public
confidence, which in legislating for a paper currency is
an element of primary importance, need not be considered at all in the regulation of a metallic currency.
The coin possesses a natural value, and therefore
may be left to find its own level ; the note possesses
no such value, and therefore must be supported by
additional contrivances.   Here, then, is the ground
upon which a discretion which has no place in the
one system, is absolutely indispensable in the other ;
for the confidence of the public in the stability of a
system resting upon convention—such as the currency—is contingent upon such a variety of circumstances, may be affected by such accidents, rumours,

and mere trifles, that nothing short of a discretion guided by full and detailed knowledge can adequately satisfy the exigencies of the case.

The further question, of course, arises as to the hands in which this discretion should be placed.* This is admittedly a point of great difficulty. I shall only, with respect to it, refer to the report of the House of Lords' Committee in the year 1848, in which the several plans proposed by witnesses are very fully examined and canvassed. One proposal, however, is decidedly

---

* The following plan, proposed by Mr. G. C Glynn, M.P., in his examination before the Lords' Committee, 1848, (Q. 1,782-5), seems deserving of attention. "If I were to offer any suggestion, I should prefer leaving the whole responsibility of the circulation in the hands of the Bank of England. I do not think there is much advantage in a double responsibility, divided between the Bank and the Government. But I consider it would be well that the Bank Court should have in it certain persons not elected by the proprietors, who should be appointed under Act of Parliament for a limited time, or in any other way which may be deemed advisable, not immediately by the Government or Proprietors, and not removable by the Government, and that they should have not an absolute veto upon the proceedings of the Bank Court, but that if they dissented from the majority, their reasons for that dissent should always be submitted in writing, and that they should be laid before Parliament, if Parliament saw fit, from time to time. I should think that the introduction of these commissioners, and their protests and influence, would exercise a very wholesome control upon the body of Governors, and at the same time would not deprive them of that power, of which, as representing the Proprietors, it would not be right that they should be deprived." "Would you add to those alterations any regulations with respect to the management of the currency with a view to the Exchanges, or to any other circumstances?—I should leave that to the Court and to those Commissioners to determine as they saw fit from time to time." "Do you consider that these Commissioners should be persons not engaged in trade?—I would rather they were not engaged in trade. I think you might find people of experience enough not engaged in trade,who were fit for the duty, but would not make it an absolute condition of eligibility." "Do you mean that they should be appointed for life?—Not for life. It is impossible to know beforehand how far a man may be fit for a position of that sort, and therefore I would make the appointment for three years, or for some period, and renewable."

negatived, viz., that of maintaining the Act, with an understanding that it should be suspended as occasion required.   Upon this the report observes, " To leave these cases, when they do arise, to be dealt with by the irregular exercise of the mere authority of the Crown and its advisers—setting aside ' once in five or six years,' or even at periods more remote, the express provisions of a distinct statute—appears wholly inconsistent with that fixity and order which it is or ought to be the object of all law to secure."

The last point to be noticed is the principle upon which the reserve of treasure, held by the Bank, should be managed.   The object of maintaining a reserve of bullion is, of course, to secure the convertibility of bank notes, and to do so with as little violence as possible to the regular transactions of commerce.   The convertibility of the note is endangered through the vicissitudes of trade, and more particularly foreign trade.   If, however, the security of the note were the only thing to be considered, a comparatively small amount of treasure would be sufficient.   Mr. Ricardo was of opinion that you might maintain a circulation of paper by bullion payments, in the proportion of £25,000,000 of paper to £3,000,000 of bullion.   Supposing such a case to be possible in theory, it could obviously be only carried out in practice by a recourse to such extreme measures on the part of the Bank, on the occurrence of the least irregularity in the exchanges, as on every such occasion to throw the commercial world into

violent convulsions. It would be necessary to resort
to a sudden contraction of the circulation ; the Bank
either refusing all accommodation to the public, or
throwing its securities in large quantities on the market ; and it is doubtless conceivable that the sudden enhancement which such measures would cause in the
value of the circulating medium, might be effectual
in saving the convertibility of the note ; though it
would be at the expense (as happened in 1847, when
measures of this kind were adopted) of great hardship
and suffering to the commercial public. Now, the
advantage of keeping a large amount of treasure in
reserve is, that we may, by availing ourselves of this
treasure in times of difficulty, secure the convertibility of our paper circulation, without being under
the necessity of resorting to expedients of this violent
and mischievous character. By holding such an
amount of treasure in the Bank in ordinary times, as
may be sufficient to meet the accidental large payments which we may have to make to foreign countries, we have a fund at hand from which we can
draw in times of pressure ; and by the assistance of
which we can tide over our seasons of difficulty with
little disturbance to the general course of trade. It
is just as if a man who had a fixed income, but
was liable to be suddenly called upon to pay large
unexpected demands, should determine to lay something by to keep as a store from which to meet
emergencies. He would by this means escape the
serious inconvenience of being obliged to make the

whole deduction from the income of the year in which
the extraordinary payment had to be made.   Just
the same is, I conceive, the principle on which the
country should maintain its reserve of bullion; and
it would seem quite as irrational on the part of the
community, as it would be on the part of an individual, if, while keeping by it this large reserve of
unproductive treasure, it prescribed rules for its conduct, which prevented it from availing itself of the
the reserve when the time of pressure came ;—if, in
short, it kept this large reserve of treasure for the
special and sole purpose of never using it.   Now this
is the way in which the present law operates: it
obliges the Bank to diminish the amount of notes
issued in proportion as its bullion is diminished ; and
as the reduction in the amount of bank notes soon
reaches the point, beyond which if carried there
would not be sufficient for the business of the country,
the effect is, that the pressure on the money market
may reach its maximum, and all commercial movements may be paralyzed, while, all the time, there
may be a large amount of unemployed treasure
locked up in the cellars of the bank.   It was in this
respect that the absurdity of the Bank Charter Act
principle became so conspicuous in the year 1847.
At that time, when the Bank had come to the end of its
legal resources,—when, for want of the usual accommodation, transactions had come to a stand-still,—the
treasure in the issue department was never reduced much
below £8,000,000.   In all probability £1,000,000 of

this sum would, any time in the month of October, have relieved the pressure, and trade would have been restored to its normal condition ; but, by the restrictive provisions of the act, this vast store of gold was rendered, when the time of need came, absolutely inefficacious, utterly unavailable for the only purpose for which a reserve fund can with any show of reason be maintained. It appears to be but common sense that, if a country goes to the expense of keeping a large surplusage of the precious metals beyond what its ordinary wants require, it should at least not be precluded, when the hour of necessity arrived, from turning this fund to account.

In this absurdity, however, the country is involved so long as the present artificial rule of restriction is maintained. We subject ourselves to all the expense of keeping a large unemployed treasure ; and we subject ourselves also to all the public inconvenience and agitation incident to those extreme measures, which are only necessary with a small one. The system unites the evils of both methods : it has the advantages of neither. What seems evidently to be the sound course, considering the vicissitudes to which commerce is liable, is to keep a large reserve of treasure, but to keep it on such an understanding as shall enable us to avail ourselves of it, when the proper occasion arrives. Instead, then, of the Bank being obliged, when a drain for gold sets in, to convulse the commercial world by a resort to extreme measures—throwing its

securities in large quantities on the market, or refusing to the public the ordinary accommodation upon
any terms,—any probable crisis may be met by the
mild expedient of a timely and gradual rise in the
rate of interest,* trusting to the export of gold ultimately to satisfy the foreign demand. This, of course,
supposes that a foreign drain is not indefinite ; but I
have already shown that it is not so.†

A proposal for the management of the Bank treasure was submitted by Mr. Tooke to the Secret
Committee of the House of Commons on Commercial
Distress, in the year 1848 ; and as in that proposal
the principles of management here advocated are fully
recognized, and have thus the sanction of Mr. Tooke's
high authority, it may not be amiss to give an outline
of his recommendations. The examination *in extenso*
would be too long to quote. He recommends that
the average amount of bullion (struck over about five
years) should be £12,000,000 ;—the maximum being
£18,000,000, the minimum £6,000,000. He would
take about four per cent. as the regular rate of interest ;
and supposing the treasure to be at its maximum
and a drain to set in, he would keep the interest at
four per cent. till the treasure was reduced to about
£12,000,000 ; as soon as the treasure fell below this,

* The advantages of this method of acting on the exchanges have been pointed
out by some of the first authorities, scientific and practical. See Mr. Tooke's
evidence before Select Committee on Banks of Issue, 1840, Q. 3753–3777.
See also Mr. Palmer's evidence before committee on Commercial Distress (House
of Commons), 1848, Q. 2034.

† See *ante* pp. 28–36.

he would raise the rate of interest to six per cent. ;
and, if the drain were not then corrected, he would
permit it to run on till the bullion was reduced to
£6,000,000. When the treasure had fallen to this,
the country would have parted with £12,000,000 of
gold ; "and I have no idea," he says, " that after
parting with £12,000,000 there are any circumstances
in which the country could be placed that would
endanger a further continuance of the drain." If,
however, the drain should continue further, he would
then let the Bank, by restricting its discounts or
otherwise, take measures for its own security ; at
worst, the evils would be no greater than under the
present system may be expected to occur upon every
serious derangement of the foreign exchanges.
Having, by acting on this rate of interest and by this
large export of gold, satisfied the drain (as in all
probable cases Mr. Tooke is satisfied would be the
result,) he would then recommend the interest to be
kept up to six per cent. till the reserve again reached
its maximum of £18.000,000   He does not say that
this should be by a regulation.'   "I am quite sure,"
he says, " that you must leave it to the discretion of
some man or some body of men.   It should
be more in the nature of an understanding, which
should come into question at the renewal of the charter of the Bank, for which they should be responsible ;
not as a matter of regulation ; for it is as a matter of
regulation that I object to the present act."

On such a plan the reserve of treasure in the bank

would perform, under our mixed currency, the same
functions which, in those countries where the currencies are metallic, are performed by the numerous
petty hoards, forming in the aggregate a very large sum,
which lie inactive in the tills and drawers of private
parties ; and which, in times of pressure, under the
temptation of high interest, come out to meet extraordinary demands ; thus saving the necessity of any
serious encroachment upon the circulating medium
of the country.   Indeed, a currency based upon such
a large reserve of treasure as Mr. Tooke has proposed,
and managed according to the principles which have
been indicated, would altogether conform much more
closely to the analogy of a metallic system (if this be
deemed a matter of great importance,) than our present monetary code ; which, in this respect at least,
fails entirely in realizing the pretensions which have
been put forward for it by its authors.